A G MAY

Build Your Author Platform Through Public Speaking

TH TSD PRESS

First edition

ISBN: 978-1-9160872-7-9

This book was professionally typeset on Reedsy.
Find out more at reedsy.com

This book is dedicated to everyone out there who is nervous of speaking in public.
Wishing you every luck in your endeavours.
You are awesome.

You can do it.

'There is nothing impossible to he (they) who will try.'

Alexander the Great
356BC - 323BC

Contents

Foreword

I'm guessing you're reading this because you've written a book and you want to promote it. Well done. Genuinely. A huge pat on the back for you. That's an amazing achievement and you should be very proud of yourself. Many people dream of writing a book, but not many actually put the hours in to make that dream a reality. It takes hard work, guts, determination and, in my case, far too much coffee and cake.

In 2016, I wrote my first book. I self-published it on Amazon. I didn't expect to sell a single copy. That's not why I wrote it. But early sales proved highly addictive, as did some lovely reviews, and soon I wanted more. Eight years on, and three books later, I have sold thousands of copies. The key to that success, for me, has been public speaking. This book will tell you how I did it.

While this text has been written with authors in mind, if you have developed a different sort of product, much of the advice in this guide will still be useful for promotion through public speaking. Please bear with all the book and writing-related references as you read on.

Whatever your route into publishing, whether traditional, independent or self-publishing, once the book is available, you want it to sell. The best way to do that is for you — the author —

to actively promote it and build your author platform. There are a great many ways to do this from Facebook ads, Amazon ads and on-line book promotional services, through book signings and radio interviews to public speaking.

In my opinion, one of the most effective way to boost book sales and reach more readers is to go out and engage with them directly. Believe it or not, one of the easiest ways to do that is through public speaking events.

When I gave my first talks I was petrified, but that didn't last. Now, I look forward to speaking at clubs and groups, as an after-dinner speaker and at many other social events. I speak for approximately forty-five minutes to an hour. After which, I connect with readers and sell books. In fact, the public speaking element of my writing business generates an income of its own alongside any book sales.

Please note: my experience relates to public speaking in the UK, both in-person and online. My preference is to speak to smaller audiences, for example 30 - 120 people. If you live in another country, another continent, or on another planet, or you wish to speak to vast stadiums full of humans, animals or extra-terrestrials, this may not be the book for you. Nevertheless, many of the principles I outline should still work, but you may have to do a little extra research and adapt measures to fit in with your local area, culture and any additional interspecies or interplanetary requirements.

This book will tell you:

- How I got into public speaking.
- How I put together a talk.
- How I overcame my nerves and did that first event; including tips for keeping anxiety flare ups under control.
- What I take to every event; my speaker's toolbox.
- How I registered on the local speaker lists and became a regular on the speaking circuit.
- Hints and tips that will help you get started promoting your book and boosting sales through public speaking.

People love a local author, but they have to know that you're there. If you don't tell anyone, how will they know?

As a public speaker, my diary is full of opportunities to reach out to new readers, make connections, build my author brand, encourage people to join my subscribers list, promote new books coming out and to sell books already published. For me, it's been a no-brainer.

1

My route into public speaking

W riting came as a complete surprise to me. Like many people, as a child I dreamed of writing a book, but never expected to do it for real. Where writing was a wonderful dream, public speaking was a nightmare. I dreaded it. Never in a million years would I ever have thought I would willingly agree to do it. Yet, now, I do it all the time and, more importantly, I enjoy it.

What changed?

A big life event propelled me to start writing. Writing then catapulted me into public speaking. To my utter amazement, I now love speaking almost as much as I love writing. Which just goes to show that we should never underestimate ourselves. With the right set of circumstances, we can achieve anything.

What triggered such a seismic shift?

Half my house fell down. That is not a euphemism. It literally happened. With no warning, the walls crumbled and nearly 80% of our home suddenly became uninhabitable. One minute it appeared fine — it obviously wasn't — and the next it was little more than a thatched roof on stilts, with disintegrating masonry below, missing windows and a constantly shifting staircase that reminded me of the Harry Potter one but with none of the magic; just boring old gravity.

Long story short. A painful six-month dispute with our house insurance company followed. They did not think that our fully comprehensive house insurance policy covered the house falling down. We disagreed. I am sure you can imagine the sorts of intense discussions that took place. In the meantime, we lived in a tent in the garden — that's my husband, myself and our four children aged 7-16. Not a lifestyle choice that I recommend.

Eventually a compromise was reached that satisfied neither our insurers nor us, but at least allowed a rebuild to start. By the time work began, we had moved into a caravan (still in the garden), which was handy, as that particular winter was very cold indeed. Eight months later, over a year after the walls fell, we moved back into our home. It had been repaired on a shoestring. We had no carpets, no curtains and barely any furniture. More to the point, we had no idea how we were going to pay back the money we'd borrowed.

Six months after that, I found myself writing a book.

From writing to speaking

For me, writing was almost as much of a surprise as the house falling. One minute I wasn't a writer and the next I was, and once I started writing, I couldn't stop. I wrote almost day and night for over a month. Soon there were nearly 60,000 words and the first draft of a book of indistinct genre and mediocre skill; a fictionalised memoir of sorts. A messy first draft, littered with bad grammar, spelling mistakes and typing howlers; but a first draft, nevertheless. Multiple re-drafts and many technique- and grammar-improving edits followed, before my book hit the Amazon bookshop shelf.

Becoming a writer was easy. It was like flicking a switch. There was a story that had to be told and it was happening whether I liked it or not.

Becoming my own publisher was slightly more complicated, but with a bit of research and some help from editors and typesetters etc, in the end, that was relatively straightforward too.

Becoming a speaker, someone with the confidence to regularly stand up in public and speak for over an hour, was something else entirely. When I was initially approached by an acquaintance from the local Women's Institute and asked if I would be interested in speaking, my initial response was a polite, but firm, *'no, thank you'*. The thought of public speaking had always terrified me. Yet, in the end, I did it, and no one is more surprised about it than I am. Not even my husband who kept giving me searching looks and asking, 'Are you sure you want to do this?' He was right to ask. Before the house fell down, if you'd suggested I stand up in front of even half a dozen people and say something I'd have been over the horizon and far away by the time you had finished your sentence.

However, the shenanigans with the house had changed me. For the first time in my life there was something I wanted to say and I was the only one who could say it. I was still scared, though, and a voice inside my head kept asking: *Why would anyone want to listen to me?*

There's a simple answer to that. Why not me?

If you've written a book, *you* are the best person to tell everyone about it. Gather your courage, and step into your spotlight. You *can* do it.

Once I had agreed to speak, I then had to put a suitable talk together. I knew in principle what my message was going to be. The problem was how communicate it in the most effective way. I'd written a book. Writing a talk couldn't be that difficult could it? Hmm. That is what the next section is all about.

2

Putting together a talk

I n my opinion, the single most effective way to engage an audience is to tell a story. People love stories and have done so since the beginning of time. Long before reading and writing were invented, our ancestors were sharing stories in caves or around campfires or hearths. Stories connect us, help us share information and learn from each other. Stories are the key to successful public speaking. And creating stories is what writers do, so you're already onto a winner.

Nevertheless, the story you are telling has to be appropriate for your audience. Are you speaking to children or adults or both? It is worth having a quick chat with whoever is booking you to speak. Ask a little bit about your audience in advance and use that information to pitch your material to the right level. If you want to be successful, and recommended on, don't assume a single talk will work as a one size fits all commodity.

My first talk was for the Women's Institute (WI). I'd been asked by an acquaintance who happened to be the speaker secretary for the group meeting. She had heard about what had happened to our house and, when a speaker dropped out at short notice, she asked if I would step in. This didn't give me much time to prepare and, while my instinctive response was one of abject terror, ever the people-pleaser, I heard myself muttering, 'Um, er... yes, okay.'

That was it. I was committed. I had to do it. I went home, kicking myself and wondering what the hell I was going to talk about. That reluctant acceptance was one of the best decisions I ever made.

What could you talk about?

Children's books

If you have written a children's book, you will find that children are very interested in where you get your ideas from and how you go about the writing process. Reading short sections out loud will always be well received. Encouraging your listeners to try writing their own stories is another excellent angle. If you can connect with a specific and age appropriate theme, especially one that chimes with the education curriculum or health and well-being, then you may find that school staff are keen to book you to talk. If you do receive a school booking, it's worth asking for some general information about the age range and/or abilities of your audience in advance, and adapt your material accordingly.

General fiction and non-fiction talk tips

Whether you write fiction or non-fiction, weaving a story-like narrative around your book will help you to make a personal connection with your audience. Tell them about your inspiration? Why does your story mean so much to you? What research did you do? Share some background on who you are and the journey you have been on. Did you travel somewhere interesting, or stay somewhere entertaining? Is there an intriguing connection, perhaps a linked theme, or an unusual element of history? Think big. Think wide. Think beyond the book.

For example: I once went to a talk where the speaker arrived with a small leather case which contained his collection of shot glasses. I hadn't checked the topic of the talk before I attended the event and if I had, I might not have gone. But, with hindsight I am very glad I did. It was fascinating. The shot glasses were antiques, going back hundreds of years and the speaker wove a magical tale about significant historic events that the precious glassware might have born witness to. It wasn't that big a leap because, hundreds of years ago, only the wealthy and powerful had drinking vessels made of glass. Those rare shot glasses genuinely could have sat on important table as kings and queens signed significant contracts and treaties, or been used to toast other important events. It was a clever, educational and engaging presentation. Had this speaker written a book on antique shot glasses, I would have been very tempted to buy a copy to give to a relative with a passion for history.

If you can't think of an original approach like the shot glass one, it doesn't matter. A more straightforward talk about writing can be absorbing too. Many people are avid readers and intrigued to know how an author goes about writing a book. On the flip side, some people hate books. (I know! As a former librarian, I don't get it either, but it's true.) Those people can't understand why anyone would waste their time reading, let alone writing a book, but even they can be intrigued by the process and what aspects you might draw on from your own life. For example, you might write action packed adventures with multiple fight scenes. If you happen to also be an Olympic-level taekwondo referee, or have a black belt in mixed martial arts, that would be a great personal story to weave into your presentation, particularly if you have associated photos or medals to display.

If you don't have a dramatic connection like that, don't worry, your audience are there to listen to whatever you want to say. Perhaps you could talk about how you developed your ideas from initial inspiration to final manuscript. Do you have any strange writing rituals? Have you suffered from writer's block and if so how did you overcome it? Are you the sort of writer who writes all night until your cat comes and sits on your laptop and forces you to stop?

If you wrote your book on post-it notes in a rusty campervan stuck up a Welsh mountain whilst on a mission to find a runaway llama, then for goodness sake, tell your audience that, and tell them why. You'll have them eating out of your hand.

Getting the balance right

When I give my 'Surviving the House That Sat Down' talk, I speak about what happened the day the house fell down, and the impact that whole disaster had. I explain how I used creativity (painting at first and then writing) as one of the ways I dealt with subsequent post-traumatic stress, which introduces powerful mental health and self-care themes that the vast majority of people are interested in and can connect with. Nevertheless, I am careful to do this in a relatively upbeat way. The last thing I want to do when I am talking is depress everyone.

Note: If you can't tell a particular story without getting triggered then it's best not to tell it at all, and definitely don't tell it if there's a chance it will trigger your audience. Spreading misery will get you nowhere fast.

Difficult material should be carefully handled. I make sure to tell a lot of light-hearted anecdotes about all the daft things that happened while we were living in a tent. It wasn't all doom and gloom, thank goodness, and the main premise of my signature talk is that when bad things happen, they are rarely all bad. Often there is something good going on at the same time, you just have to look very hard to find it.

People want to hear about the good things. The overcoming of life's obstacles. They want to know everything will be okay. If you can give them that, you are on to a winning presentation and your audience will be clamouring for your book and/or recommending you on as a speaker.

Promoting your book

If anyone has any experience of creative writing classes, or professional editorial reports, you will no doubt have heard the phrase that writers should show and not tell. I'm not completely convinced of that particular pearl of wisdom. I believe good writing involves a careful balance of both elements. Nevertheless, I do think showing and not telling is essential when giving a speech. Don't tell them they *have* to buy your book. Be subtle. Show them why they want it, instead. If you can deftly weave your book into the whole entertaining experience, without your audience realising it, you will have written a successful promotional talk.

Avoid any form of hard sell. It puts people off and you won't get invited back or recommended on. By all means mention your book, in passing (and let it be known where copies can be bought) but don't make it the main attraction. Believe me, no matter how much you love your book, it can't possibly be so amazing that talking about it will sustain the interest of a room full of people for more than a few minutes.

Finding your hook

If you've ever pitched your manuscript to an agent, you'll know that you need to have a hook for your book in order to get their attention. Like your elevator pitch (see page 19 for more details), your hook is a way to reel someone in using only a few words.

It's the same with a talk. You need something tangible that tells people what your talk is about without rambling off on a tangent. The right hook for a presentation won't necessarily be the precise hook you use for your book, but its purpose will be the same. As is often the case when writing your manuscript, the hook for your talk may not become apparent until you've written a fair amount of material, so be prepared to write several drafts before you get the talk and thus the hook right.

Think of a catchy title

If you can get your talk's hook into your talk's title, so much the better. Bear in mind that a speaker secretary looking to book talks for a group will looking for something interesting and engaging. They might have been recommended a long list of titles. Your title needs to stand out. It should be succinct and attention grabbing, and make people think, '*I want to listen to that.*'

The title of my signature talk, '*Surviving the House That Sat Down,*' does exactly that. It raises a question in the reader's mind and makes them want to know more. The fact that my book's title is similar is a bonus, but that is not necessarily the reason people ask me to speak.

The finale

A well-rehearsed, punchy ending to your presentation is a good idea, preferably something that will stick in your audience's hearts and minds for all the right reasons. Whatever you do, try to end your talk on a positive note.

There is no harm in the end of your talk including some sort of call to arms, such as *'here's where you can buy my book, if you are interested', 'please leave a review,'* or *'please join my email list'.* This doesn't have to be as militant or in-your-face as it sounds. Let people know if you have brought copies of your books. Perhaps mention your website, or any freebies you have to give away. Keep it short and sweet, but don't forget it.

I like to suggest that people might want to join my creatives list to receive my (rather intermittent) newsletters with details of my writing progress, any new books being published or the latest painting videos I'm releasing on YouTube.

If you are happy to take questions, then the end of your talk is an obvious time to do so.

Answering questions

There are a number of things to consider when handling questions at a public speaking event.

It's useful to tell your audience in the early stages of your talk whether they will have an opportunity to ask questions and when that will be. This stops people interrupting at random intervals which, if you are new to public speaking, can break your concentration.

Questions are a good thing, so don't be afraid of them. It shows that your audience were listening and are keen to know more. I used to be scared of questions, and thought that I wouldn't know the answer. This is an understandable concern but, remember, you are talking about **your** book. You wrote it. If you don't know the answer, no one will. Anticipating the type of question that may come up is a smart way to calm your nerves. You can rehearse possible answers much as you rehearse your talk, so that they come easily to mind when certain points are raised. Make eye contact with the person asking the question, but don't feel you have to rush into the answer. Pausing to reflect is perfectly acceptable, as is making sure you understand the question properly.

More on questions and potential interruptions or heckling later.

Afterwards

After questions, you will need to hand the focus of the audience back to the event host. You could tell your audience that you hope they have enjoyed themselves and thank them for listening. Even if they weren't a brilliant audience, it doesn't hurt to say that they were. The best way to engage successfully is to be friendly, positive and chatty. People buy into people. If they like you, there's a good chance they'll buy your book, either for themselves or for someone else.

3

Other considerations when speaking

Once you have written your talk, the next thing to think about is how you deliver it. The style with which you present your material can have a huge impact on how your message is received. Good opening sections and good closing sections are essential. If you get a bit boggy in the middle, that's okay. As with many things in life, you can get away with a bit of fudging if you start well and end well.

The emotional journey

Like a novel, an effective talk will take the audience on a journey. As writers we often use the opening chapters of a novel to set the 'rules' for the story and the world in which that story will operate. A presentation always benefits from clear direction too, and opening with a quick verbal map can help your audience relax and feel secure. It is also a good way to set the tone. For example, your verbal map could be as basic as saying the following:

"Hello. I am delighted to be here today to share my story about....
In the next forty minutes, I plan to talk a little bit about my childhood and how I always wanted to ... (insert dream... e.g. to be a writer, perhaps?) ... but didn't know how to achieve it, then one day ... (an amazing thing happened) ... and this led to ... (an unexpected development) ... and now I am one. Yay!!! Let me tell you all about it..."

A careful balance of emotional ups and downs throughout your talk will help to bring your listeners on board with your story. Although, for obvious reasons, it's a good idea to end on an 'up'.

I try to include a few humorous anecdotes in my opening paragraphs to let my listeners know that it is okay to laugh even if my overall theme is a serious one.

Setting the pace

Pacing is important. You have your foot on the throttle. You have complete control over how things unfold. Take your time, make sure your words are clear and that your audience can hear you. Try not to gabble, but don't speak so slowly that you send your audience to sleep, either. Changing the pace during your presentation and/or emphasising certain elements of your story, can help to keep your listeners focussed.

You can use your voice in different ways; such as increasing or decreasing your volume, or altering the speed at which you speak. However, do keep these changes appropriate to the material you are discussing at the time, otherwise it could come across as a bit strange.

Just as you would appeal to different senses when writing — especially if you write fiction — you can do the same when speaking. People process things in a multitude of different ways, for example, some prefer audible information where others prefer visual information. The same could be said for texture, taste and smell. A talk is, by its very nature, audible, nevertheless there are thing you can do to bring in the other senses. This might include passing something around your audience for them to touch and/or smell.

In my case, I use my art work to illustrate my talks. Sometimes I hand around small original paintings for people to see close up. I also find interspersing sections of talking with short video clips showing a painting in progress is a useful way keep people's attention.

However, don't get bogged down with gimmicks. Everything in your presentation needs to have a purpose. That purpose is to enhance your audience's experience and keep their focus on you and your message.

Authenticity

It helps if your talk can reflect something of you and what you are trying to achieve with your book. Simon Sinek did a great TED talk on How Great Leaders Inspire Action. You can find a recording of the talk on the TED YouTube channel. It is well worth checking out even though it is about business and products. The basic principles are the same for books. Think about why you have written your book. Why do you think someone would want to read it? What are the themes? Are they themes you feel really strongly about.

When I give my signature talk, I am not really speaking about the house (although superficially I am) I'm actually talking about the importance of building resilience and how essential it is to practice self-care when life gets tough.

PowerPoint or no PowerPoint?

Using technology in your presentation can be a helpful tool. If you are going to use one, bear in mind that the best presentations use images rather than text, something relevant for the audience to look at while they listen to you.

Definitely avoid using thousands of slides with lots of tiny print. These get tedious very fast, often sending audiences to sleep. Text based slides can divert your audience's attention away from you because people need to focus to read them. This is particularly damaging if they read ahead of whatever you're talking about and then stop listening altogether. Thus, it's advisable to avoid giving your audience mixed messages. Be clear. Either you want them to focus on the slides or you want them to focus on you.

As a general rule, your talk should be able to stand on its own two feet without visual aids. That way, if you have a technical issue like your projector failing or the venue having a power cut, your talk can go ahead regardless.

Elevator pitch

If you are a good speaker, the speaker secretary may ask if you have other talks in your repertoire. An elevator pitch is a quick two to three sentence summary that explains each of your talks in a clear, appealing way. It's worth having a few elevator pitches available for that moment when a speaker secretary or other contact asks you what you can offer.

For example, if I were speaking to a potential social club contact, I might say that I am a huge advocate of the importance of creative activities as effective tools for self-care and that my signature talk and my follow-up talk both reflect that theme.

Alternatively, if I were taking to a business contact, I might say that I give practical tips on speaking in public so that clients can build their brand and boost sales.

4

Getting started and finding bookings

Developing your ideas

I t is always a good idea to start by giving a few talks to a sympathetic audience. I have a group of friends who volunteered to sit through my talk during the development stages. In exchange for a glass of wine and some pizza, they gave me constructive feedback which enabled me to consolidate an effective presentation. I'd never been so nervous in my life before but, in spite of that, it was a fun evening with a lot of laughter and, afterwards, I was able to polish my presentation.

This phase is especially useful, if you are able to practice before representatives of your target readership. If you have a friendly contact for a local group that fits that bill, they might be willing (particularly if you aren't asking for a speaker fee) to let you give a trial talk to their members who will give you feedback on how it went and practical suggestions on how to improve.

Making contact

If you don't have friends or acquaintances in suitable local clubs or groups to ask for contact details, you can still find details by running an internet search. Many groups have websites that include a comments box. Send a polite message inquiring about whether they are looking for speakers and letting them know what you can offer. Remember to include your email address so that they can reply. You don't necessarily need to provide a phone number at this stage, and can judge if you are comfortable to do that based on the response you receive. If no one replies, you haven't lost anything but a few minutes of your time.

If you are promoting a children's book you might wish to approach schools and or children's clubs. With schools, you could ring reception using the number advertised on the school website. Ask for the name and email address of an appropriate member of staff. Note that many members of staff in schools wear multiple hats, so you could end up contacting a variety of different people such as the school librarian, the head of English, the special educational needs coordinator (SENCO), the well-being officer or any other member of staff. The school calendar is put together during the summer term for the year ahead with little to no wiggle room to shoehorn changes in later on. It is worth being ready to approach school staff between the Easter holiday and the May half term to maximise your chances of success for bookings in the following academic year.

Most libraries run author events as well. Pop into your local library and ask who to contact. The librarian should be able to let you know which libraries in the area have the space to hold book events. With luck they will have a contact email address to give you. Children's events are particularly popular during school holidays and at weekends.

Local book shops (especially independent book shops) often hold author-led events. Again, these may depend on whether the shop has sufficient room for a gathering. My local Waterstones were happy to have a book signing for me, and delighted that I could offer a twenty-minute presentation for their customers too. Success on this front is entirely down to the individual stores, but if you don't ask it won't happen. So, why not give it a try?

Word of mouth

Don't underestimate the power of the grapevine. Good speakers are valued on many levels. If you give a good talk, word will spread.

The title and subject matter of my first talk, *Surviving the House That Sat Down* was intriguing enough to get me a couple of initial bookings. These went well and thanks to word of mouth my reputation as a speaker took over and, soon, I was receiving multiple requests to speak.

Pace yourself

Speaking events can be tiring. It's not just the time you spend in front of your audience that causes this. You have to load your car with boxes of books (and maybe a projector and laptop etc.) then drive to the venue, park up (hopefully nearby), unload, set up, speak, network afterwards and sell books, pack up, reload the car, drive home, unpack the car again and tidy things away. You may only speak for half an hour or forty-five minutes at an event, and it may only be fifteen minutes from your house, but that might still involve three hours of work or more.

I often return from evening events and find I can't sleep straight away. This usually happens if an event has gone particularly well. It's a good idea to build in some relaxation time and also to make sure you have something readily available to eat and drink when you get home.

Beware, no matter how well the event goes, the day afterwards you might feel a little deflated. This is quite normal. Speaking in front of people uses a lot of adrenaline. In addition to any physical exhaustion from carting boxes of books around, you may find your body chemistry takes time to return to normal too. Be kind to yourself. Don't overload your schedule.

I limit bookings to three or four speaking events a month, as this works well with my other writing and painting commitments. I am often booked at least eighteen months in advance, but by not overloading my schedule, if a local event comes up at short notice — perhaps another speaker has had to cancel — I can usually squeeze them in. Local events are my favourite, because there is limited travel time and they don't impact too much on all the other things I am juggling. Plus, speaker secretaries are always grateful if you fill in at short notice, and your details are more likely to be shared on as someone who is happy to help.

Don't forget

Have a business card or something similar that you can hand out with your contact details. Every talk you give is an opportunity for someone to hear you and then recommend you on to another group. If you are good enough, word will spread. You may not even have to do much advertising in order to get bookings.

Business cards are not quite so useful for children's events. However, a free book mark would be a good alternative. Or, you might wish to hand out a colouring sheet at the end. Perhaps one based around the art on your book cover. Include your name, book title and website details at the bottom of the sheet for reference.

5

Anxiety and public speaking

There are a number of things you can do to reduce anxiety associated with public speaking.

Overcoming physical nerves on the day

The brain is incredibly elastic and constantly open to learning new things. It is possible to re-program your responses to certain situations. Fortunately, public speaking is one of those situations.

When I gave my first couple of talks, I used to get terribly nervous. My heartbeat would increase, I'd feel giddy and sick, I would perspire and have shaky hands.

Over time, I learned that while these are all symptoms of nerves, they are also symptoms of excitement. It is easy to confuse the two.

It was understandable that you get a physical reaction if you are standing on a stage with hundreds of people staring at you and expecting you to say something not only coherent but hopefully entertaining. Alarm bells are bound to start clanging away. Nevertheless, it is possible to change your reaction by taking control of the narrative that's going on inside your head. I can't tell you how or why this works, but I know that it does, because I've done it.

When I started feeling nervous before a speaking event, I told myself that it was because I was excited to be able to share my story. By repeating that narrative, I began to calm down. Before long I was genuinely experiencing excitement and looking forward to going on stage.

Be prepared

Make time to practice. You need to know your material.

Don't practice it in your head. Practice it out loud, so that both your mouth and your brain are fully engaged and working together. Running through vague concepts in your mind isn't enough. To be fully prepared you need to actually say the words and/or variations of sentences that you will actually use out loud. This will ensure the words you want are readily available to you when you need them and you don't have to go searching for them. It also massively reduces what I call the um-factor.

There's nothing more likely to turn your audience off than you spending most of the talk saying um…um…um as you fumble for the right words.

Having said that, I strongly advise against learning your talk word for word. Reciting material parrot-fashion sounds wrong and you will lose any emotional connection with your listeners. Nevertheless, you need to know where you are going and how you plan to get there. It is essential to be familiar enough with your material that you are not stumbling over your words and are able to keep going under pressure.

It can help to write your talk in sections that can be swapped around if necessary and have extra material ready that you can transition into if the situation calls for it. You might be asked to speak for longer than you were originally booked for due to a change in line up and its useful to have something coherent to say.

It's also useful to have a few safe anecdotes you can slip into if you lose your thread, giving you time to recover your bearings and get back on track. Most of the time your audience needn't know this is happening.

I always have a complete run-through of my talk the day before. My neighbours probably think I'm weird because I walk up and down the garden talking to myself. Alternatively, if I have time, I might go out for a walk. Fortunately, we live in the countryside. If I stop to talk to wild ponies, birds, or cows peering over hedges, there's no one but the occasional tractor driver or cyclist to notice. I'm not totally bonkers, I just find it helps to have the words I am going to need in the fore-front of my mind before I give a talk and saying them out loud in various arrangements beforehand is an excellent way to achieve this.

Be organised

I like to check my speaker toolkit (see later section on equipment to see what is included in this) before I leave, to make sure everything is working and that I haven't forgotten anything. This helps me stay calm. Knowing that everything functions and that I have a backup (again see later information) available in the event of a power failure, means I can relax and look forward to the event. I always arrive early, having checked my route in advance. I have a paper map in my car in the event that my satnav fails or the event is in such a remote area that there is no internet and/or no phone signal.

I usually look for is a coffee shop or pub nearby, so that if I am too early I can sit somewhere quiet and run through my talk. Practicing my introductory statements right before the event means they are fresh in my mind and increases my chances of making a powerful start. If there is nowhere suitable to stop off on route, I will sit in the car at the venue and practice there.

Expectations

Managing other people's expectations about your presentation is important. Be clear about what you can offer. I am not the sort of person that can have a microphone lobbed at her with half a moment's notice, not if I'm going to say anything remotely profound or entertaining. I need plenty of warning, time to get into the right headspace, a familiar topic and a time limit at the very least. For me, off the cuff is off the cards and I have no shame in admitting that.

6

Book sales at speaking events

Not every event will automatically result in immediate sales. Most will, but some don't. Lack of physical book sales at an event can be for any number of reasons and don't necessarily reflect on your ability as a speaker. Both paperback and e-book sales can come in days, weeks or months after an event.

There is much more happening during your presentation than mere book sales. You are showcasing yourself, growing your profile and making valuable connections. Every single person you speak to whether in a group or individually is a potential reader or a conduit to other readers. You never know, someone who doesn't read your genre, might still consider your book a good present for someone else.

If you are speaking as part of a whole day of programmed event, the placement of your session within the timetable may affect the overall audience response. For example, are you speaking just before lunch? If so, everyone might be ravenous and more interested in diving for the lunch queue after you finish than coming to buy your book. Then again, if you speak straight after lunch, your audience might be ready for a quick nap and you'll have to politely ignore a degree of snoring. There's no point getting upset over the running order for such an event, just do the best you can. Don't stomp off in a huff and lock yourself in the loo to cry. Instead, make sure you make the most of any opportunity to chat and network in the scheduled breaks. Have a freebie to give away like a book mark or a business card.

If you build a good reputation on the speaker circuit, as someone who is in demand, as well as adaptable and easy to work with, you will soon be in a position to politely request your preferred speaking slot from individual organisers when they approach you.

Other reasons for lack of sales on the day might include the organiser forgetting to remind audience members that merchandise is available, or attendees might simply not have brought their wallets with them. It happens. Chalk it up to experience and don't take it personally.

7

Improving your listeners' experience

There are a number of ways to ensure that your presentation is received well by those listening to you.

Connecting with your audience

Pitching your talk at the right level is essential. Make sure you use appropriate language and material. Tone and manner are important as well. It is vital that you don't come across as patronising. Never assume you are brighter than your audience. You might be an authority on a subject, but that doesn't mean your listeners are less intelligent than you. You will lose any sympathy if your audience think you are full of yourself.

Speaking about your own feelings is important to connect on an emotional level, but never tell you audience how *they* should feel.

Drawing a response from your listeners early on help them to engage. For example, I often speak to social groups where the average age is between fifty and seventy. One of my talks involves the mention of Weebles, a small wobbly toy that was hugely popular in the 1970's. I usually ask if anyone can remember the jingle. This always gets a response. Most people laugh and several chant 'Weebles wobble but they don't fall over.' Bringing up a positive childhood memory in this way lifts the mood in the room and, afterwards, I can feel that my listeners are more attentive.

Keep it real

Make sure you are not talking _at_ your audience. Talking _with_ or _to_ them is much better. I was lucky enough to recognise the difference quite early on in my speaking career, but the realisation came about by accident. I had arrived at an event almost late. Note, I say almost. I cannot stand being late. This near disaster was enough to throw me off my game. As I stood up to speak, very flustered, I realised I hadn't got my brain in the right gear. As I scrabbled around inside my head for what I had planned to say and failed to find the thread to start, I was on the point of panic. Then, I looked at my audience and saw it was all women like me and, for some reason, I relaxed and started to speak as I would to a friend over a coffee. I opened up about how I had really felt about living in a tent in the garden with my children, not knowing where to turn to find a way forward. I was completely honest about how scared I'd been, whilst also telling little stories about how amazing the children had been throughout the whole disaster.

That wouldn't necessarily have worked with every audience, but it did with that one. I was talking to mothers, to sisters, to aunts and grandmas, all women familiar with the heartache and love that goes into holding families of all shapes and sizes together through all sorts of disasters. What I was sharing was real, and my audience sat up and listened. I think it is interesting to note, that day I sold more books than ever before.

Always, always speak from the heart.

I think the best way to achieve this is to speak as if you know that there is at least one person in the room who really needs to hear what you have to say. You don't know who that person is, which is why you must address the whole room, but this mindset will help you come across in a genuine way.

Don't stare at the floor or over everyone's heads, while pretending they aren't there. Mentally divide your audience into sections; front left, front right, middle left, middle right and then back left and right. During your talk, make sure you allow your gaze to drift over each of these sections in turn, looking at the faces of the people listening. You don't have to make proper eye contact, in fact it's better if you don't because you don't want to make anyone feel uncomfortable by appearing to stare at them, but do acknowledge that there are real people out there as this will increase your authenticity.

Try videoing yourself and watching it back

I know it sounds utterly hideous, but recording yourself speaking is a useful activity. You can pick up all sorts of bad habits by reviewing both video and audio footage of you speaking. Try watching with the sound turned off to check your body language and then try listening without the picture to pick up on verbal issues.

In the early days, I had a habit of beginning almost every sentence with 'now', and the word 'actually' cropped up with annoying regularity too. I wasn't aware of it at the time, but when I listened to the recording, it was as grating as someone playing a recorder with loads of enthusiasm but no idea how to stay in tune.

The other thing I hadn't thought about was the way I was standing. I had a habit of standing with my weight on one leg with the other leg crossed over at the ankle. I felt quite stable and relaxed standing this way and had no idea that it made me look like I needed the toilet. As soon as it was pointed out to me, I checked the video and I could see it for myself. These days I stand with my weight evenly distributed, my feet hip-width apart, my back straight, my knees slightly bent and my shoulders back. I look my audience in the eye. There is nothing about my stance that will stop my audience from engaging with what I am staying.

Don't stress yourself out trying to make people laugh.

Humour can help with listener engagement, but it isn't essential and of course should always be appropriate to your audience and subject matter. You don't have to be a stand-up comedian to be a public speaker. You don't have to tap dance, juggle or eat fire, but, you do need to be interesting. If you can get people to laugh, that's a bonus. One of the best ways to help your audience enjoy your presentation, is for you to enjoy delivering it. This will come with practice and confidence.

During my first years as a speaker, I gave my presentation to many different audiences. It was fascinating to note all the different reactions I received. It was possible to work out the elements of my talk that were humorous from audience responses and I deliberately polished those sections to gain laughs or lighten the mood when needed. For some reason, whenever I take the mickey out of my husband, it always gets a laugh. It's always done in good faith and, fortunately, he thinks it's funny too. Or, at least, that's what he says…

8

What if your talk is met by deathly silence?

The old adage: 'don't judge a book by its cover' works for audiences too. It's not always possible to judge how an audience is receiving your presentation by looking at them. Don't let a false narrative in your head undermine your time on stage. Stay calm and steady and keep talking.

During one particular event, a member of the audience frowned at me the entire time I was speaking. This could have derailed me if I had let it. Fortunately, I had the presence of mind to divert my focus to a group of people who seemed positively engaged and kept going. However, at the end of my talk, it was with some trepidation that I realised the frowning person was approaching me. To my surprise, he told me it was one of the most interesting presentations he had ever heard. He was a really nice person, it just turns out that he had a grumpy listening face.

On another occasion, the audience was so silent that if I wasn't looking right at them, I'd have thought they'd all left the room. Again, I nearly stopped talking, I was so convinced I'd lost them. Nevertheless, I soldiered on, telling my story as if to myself, and finally limped into my closing section, desperate to pack up and be gone. As I handed the microphone back to the club president, I got the shock of my life when thunderous applause broke out. Apparently, the silence was due to everyone being so hooked by my story that they were hanging off my every word. What I took for disinterest was total absorption, and I had no idea.

In both cases, the subsequent Q&A sessions were interesting and great fun.

9

What to consider when accepting a booking

C learly you need to know basics like day, date, time, location and which talk you are giving (if you have several) when you accept a booking, but there are also a number of other things you should consider.

Directions

Check that you know where you are going well in advance. Double check postcodes and maps. People organising events make mistakes like the rest of us. I once had a lady give me her home postcode not the venue's postcode and if I hadn't checked before I left home, my satnav would have taken me to the wrong village.

Ask if there is any specific information you need to know. For example, if the venue is on a one-way street that can only be approached from the north on a Tuesday afternoon in October. Or, perhaps the car park is in the next county in an overgrown railway siding that doubles as grazing for a herd of grouchy llamas. These are facts you need to know.

I am, of course, being facetious, but for peace of mind, finding your venue is not something to wing at the last minute. Driving around in circles in the middle of nowhere in the dark looking for a non-existent village hall isn't just annoying, it can be quite alarming. Arriving late, panicked and half out of your mind with frustration isn't conducive for a good speaking experience, for either you or your audience.

Communication

An email address and a contact telephone number are essential information to request when accepting a booking. In addition, ask for a mobile number that will be switched on and monitored on the day of the event. That way, if you run into trouble you have someone you can contact.

Transport

For the vast majority of events you will need to be able to get to the venue under your own steam. At a push, you might get an organiser to pick you up from the local bus or train station if you are using public transport, but many won't and it will limit your bookings.

Do ask your organiser about parking. Most groups will reserve a parking spot for you as close as possible to the venue if they can. Nevertheless, this isn't always possible and sometimes you might have to pay for parking. It is as well to know these things in advance.

Equipment

Your venue may provide all the equipment you will need to give your talk. If you are using a PowerPoint you may merely need to email them your file in advance or bring a thumb drive with you. It is worth asking ahead of time.

On the other end of the scale, you might need to bring everything that you will need with you. I take a speaker kit to every event, just in case the equipment provided by the venue fails and I need a backup. See my checklist in Appendix 1.

My basic speaker kit includes:

- Laptop
- Connection/adapter cable
- Wireless clicker to change slides
- Projector
- Screen
- 4 metre extension cable with multiple sockets

- Small portable microphone and battery pack

The other things I take include:

- A box of books for sale.
- A sign saying how much.
- A pen to sign books if requested.
- Business cards/book marks
- A float for those paying cash.

Note: You may also wish to get set up to take card payments. Speak to your bank about how best to do this.

Most venues will provide a table for equipment or books.

If you are at a large venue or part of a whole day event it might be acceptable for you to bring other products for sale, as well, but you would need to check with the organiser in advance.

If you are speaking to smaller clubs and groups, do be careful that you don't give the impression that you are setting up a shop. These clubs are often run as charities and have very strict rules about what you can and can't do. Also, be aware that they may ask for a percentage of sales to be donated to them, so do your research. In addition, often these clubs have hired the venue for a short period of time and they need to be finished and out in a timely fashion after the event is over. Whatever you bring should be quick and easy to pack away.

I have a couple of decorated wooden boxes, one for cards and one for books. These have lids to protect the contents from the rain when loading and unloading. They look pretty and appealing on a table. At the end of the event, I simply shut the box lids, stack them onto a small wheeled trolley along with my other equipment and, within a couple of minutes, I am ready to leave.

10

Finances

Money is always something to be considered when you start speaking in public. Will the event be a paid speaking event, or not? Some are, some aren't. The difficulty can be working out which is which. The only way to find out is to be polite and upfront and ask if the booking is for a paid speaking event. There are benefits to both paid and unpaid events and it is entirely up to you whether you wish to accept the booking or not.

Remember to keep a record of the income and expenditure associated with your talks and book sales in order to declare the information on your tax return. Advice from an accountant might prove useful.

Speaker fee

Many social groups expect to pay their speakers. Nevertheless, one difficulty you might have is working out what to charge. If you are unsure, you could mention a figure as a starting point, but be prepared to adjust that based on the response you get. For example, you could say that you generally charge a basic rate of £100. (I have just picked a random figure here. Your charge is entirely up to you.) Make sure you follow up that figure by mentioning that if this doesn't suit their budget you occasionally offer talks at a reduced rate to new groups and then ask them what their budget will stretch to. This information will allow you to decide if you wish to speak at the lower rate or not.

If, however, you feel that you pitched your original figure too low, then you could try raising it for the next group and see what response you get. It's important not to come across as money-grabbing, but also important that you feel you are receiving a reasonable return for your efforts.

As for those events that do not include a speaker fee at all, you need to decide if you wish to speak anyway. I think giving talks for free is fun. There is less pressure involved and they are a good opportunity to make connections, and if you can sell books afterwards, then that has to be a win.

Take your time and judge each opportunity on its merits and decide what you want to achieve from it.

Mileage

Always check how far you will have to travel and if you have to pay for parking. See if your host will cover your mileage/parking and at what rate. For example, many of the events I am booked for will provide free parking and have an accepted flat fee for mileage which at the time of writing this book is around the 0.35 pence per mile mark. It's not a huge amount, but does go a little way towards fuel and wear and tear on my car.

Don't forget to multiply your mileage by 2 to include travel both to and from the event. This would be in in addition to any speaker fee and should be agreed in advance.

Payment

If you are speaking under your author name but your real name is on your bank account, you need to apprise your host of this information. Make it clear that payment, whether by BACS or cheque, needs to be made out to the right name. An invoice with payment details sent in advance helps to ensure this, but be advised that it is rare to be paid in advance of an event. If you do send your invoice in advance, make it clear that you are merely sending it for the attention of the group's treasurer so that they will have all the information they need for payment on the day and highlight the fact that the account name you need payment made to is different from your author name.

Insurance.

Some venues won't have you as a speaker unless you can prove you have public liability insurance (PLI).

Consider getting a PAT — portable appliance test — done for any electronic equipment you are supplying, as this will work in conjunction with your PLI to protect you against potential problems arising in the case of an accident occurring. An internet search for providers local to you will offer contact details, as will your local check-a-trade (and similar) website. Most insurance companies will offer PLI, although it is interesting to note that the Society of Authors (at the time of writing) offers a discount on PLI for book related events as part of their Membership Plus scheme.

If you are driving to paid events and have equipment and books in your car it is worth checking with your car insurance company in case you need to be covered for business use.

11

Building your author platform

By far and away the best way to build your author platform through public speaking is to deliver an outstanding presentation that has everyone going away talking about it and telling their friends that they absolutely *have* to hear you. I'm not kidding. This really works. A relaxed, fun, interesting talk delivered with panache and — even better — an uplifting message, will have everyone passing your name along and will also trigger more bookings.

Social media

Post about your talks on social media. You can comment about ordering in books to sell, or packing the car. Take a picture of the venue. Take a selfie with some of the wonderful people you meet, although remember to get their permission before posting online. Make sure to mention that your book is selling well. If you don't want to sound like you are showing off, be oblique about it. Say that you have to order more copies in because you have sold out. That could lead onto another post of the new books arriving and you unpacking them. Perhaps you could chat about the best question an audience member asked and then give your answer. Be creative. Mention that more information is available in your profile. Put a link to your website in your profile.

Website

List the talks you offer on your website and have a contact form for people to inquire about booking. Include photos or even short videos of events you have spoken at. A list of the types of clubs and groups you have visited is also useful. This will give anyone searching for a speaker an idea of what you offer.

A subscription box on your website, where interested people can sign up to receive your newsletter or other such communication, is a great tool for building a following. This will enable you to announce any new releases (of both talks and books) directly to your readership. Make sure that your website is GDPR compliant if you are storing people's personal details.

At the end of your talk, remember to mention your website. I always notice an increase in subscribers after an event.

Speaker profile

A speaker profile is a document you can email out to anyone inquiring about your talks. It should include your email and/or mobile number, social media links, website, some relevant information about you, a list of the talks you offer, a list of previous groups you have spoken for and quotes from positive reviews if you have them. A headshot on your profile is useful, too. I wouldn't include details of your speaker fee on your profile. It will give you no room to manoeuvre. Costs can be discussed once someone comes back with a potential booking.

Radio/newspaper

If you are sending a press release out to your local radio station or newspaper about your book as part of your publication publicity package, mention that you are a public speaker and available to visit schools, clubs and groups. Include your talk title, especially if it includes a great hook.

12

Security

A lways give careful thought to your personal safety and take sensible precautions.

Generally, the clubs and groups I speak for promote their pre-booked events within the reach of their own network and there is no need for me to drum up any additional interest unless I want to. This means that I rarely advertise my speaking events in advance on-line, especially if they are late at night, or in remote areas.

However, you might be put in a position where you are actively driving ticket sales for an event yourself and therefore announcing to the world exactly where and when you will be, so be aware of your personal safety. This might be particularly important if you are arriving or leaving an event on your own late at night, or if you are carrying a float or cash from book sales. Make a sensible judgement call in such circumstances and take appropriate steps to stay safe.

13

Audience participation

Getting your audience actively engaged in your talk is the best way to build a positive atmosphere. Ask an obvious question. Chose something that can be answered in the affirmative. For example, 'Who here likes reading?' or 'Give me a show of hands, if you have ever thought about writing a book?'

If no one responds, don't worry, the answer is irrelevant to your talk really, and you can always pretend someone smiled or waved discretely at you. The audience are all looking at you, not at each other, so no one will know. Simply scan the crowd, smile and nod, and then carry on.

As your confidence grows you might ask genuine questions that give audience members a chance to give an opinion or open up about themselves. Remember to build time into your talk to allow for this, and have some backup material in case they are all too shy to speak.

Q&A sessions

Many speaking engagements will involve a Q&A session at the end. This was the thing that scared me most about presenting when I started out. I worried about what people might ask. What if I couldn't think quickly enough to respond coherently? What if I didn't know the answer at all? I was afraid of looking stupid, which is a perfectly natural response.

It's okay to take a few seconds (even twenty) to think about a question. You can also buy yourself more time by saying something like, 'Gosh, that's a good question.' The questioner will feel flattered that you have complemented their question, regardless of how mundane it actually is. You could repeat the question as if making sure you've got it right. Such delaying tactics give you space to formulate a reply whilst still engaging with the audience.

Sometimes your questioner will ramble around the point, giving you a chance to pick out a question from what they say, preferably the question you want to answer.

It's fine to admit you don't know something, and often preferable to making something up. I find it's rare to get a question that stumps me. I am usually talking about my books, myself and my experiences. Who knows about all that better than me?

If you do get a tricky question, you can always suggest that the person who has asked it comes to see you afterwards, and then move on. This gives you time to think of a reply and takes away the pressure of everyone looking at you while do it.

As with most things, practice that makes things easier. The best way to get good at Q&A sessions is to do them. You'll find that the same sorts of questions come up time after time and you'll get very good at fielding whatever is thrown at you.

Heckling

In my experience heckling does happen, but it is rare. It can take the form of someone actively talking to you during your presentation. They don't have to have any sinister intent, and might just be asking a question, which can easily be answered or deflected for later by saying, 'I'm coming on to that in a minute,' or, 'do you mind asking me that at the end?' The important thing is not to let interruptions throw you.

Alternatively, someone might be intentionally trying to derail you. If that is the case, you could look to see if the event organiser is likely to step in. If not, it's your decision whether to acknowledge the interruption or not. No one will blame you if you don't.

Some interruptions can be more passive and might, for example, involve people in the audience talking to each other. This is rude, but it happens. My suggestion is to keep calm and keep talking. It might take a while before they stop causing a disruption but stick to your guns. Pretend they aren't there. In most cases, someone near the rude people will tell them to pipe down or leave.

There are some great articles on-line about how to deal with hecklers. I suggest doing some research and deciding how you think you would prefer to handle things.

14

After your talk

After you finish your talk, be prepared for people to want to chat to you. Many will thank you, even if they don't buy your book. They may have a story of their own to share with you. Remember that, depending on how quickly the event organiser expects you to pack up and leave, having a chat with people after you've finished speaking is an important part of the process. It is an opportunity to make connections for future sales and event bookings. Hopefully, someone will also provide you with a cup of tea and a slice of cake, at the very least. One can always hope...

In the event that your talk has gone as brilliantly as it possibly could, you might find that there is a bit of a rush of people wanting to speak to you afterwards.

However, if no one approaches you after you leave the stage, don't take it personally. It doesn't mean that your talk went badly. There may be other attractions on offer. After a polite interval —drink your tea and eat your biscuit — start putting your equipment away. Pack your books last, in case anyone wanders over right at the end.

Comfort yourself with the knowledge that some events simply do not result in sales on the day. That doesn't mean that you won't get e-book sales, or bookings for more events.

Once you get home, it is a good idea to send an email to the person who booked you to thank them for having you. This is the point at which you can send additional information about further talks you offer and is a great opportunity to remind them of the links to your book and website.

15

How I Launched myself on the local speaker circuit

L ocal social clubs and groups were the key to my successful launch onto the speaker circuit. There are a huge number and variety of social clubs to choose from. The list of possible groups you could speak for is as long as you want it to be, but it will require research on your part to narrow down those events that work for your book. Some of the groups I have spoken for in the past include:

- The Women's Institute
- The Towns Women's Guild
- Probus
- Round Circle
- Inner Wheel
- Ladies Circle
- University of the 3rd Age (U3A)
- Live Laugh Love Ladies Clubs

- Various lunch and dinner clubs
- Social clubs like sailing clubs, bowling clubs, book clubs, writing clubs and art clubs
- CAMEO
- The local medical society
- Business groups
- Networking groups.

Making connections

If you have any friends or neighbours involved in a social group, you could ask for an introduction or for contact details of the speaker secretary. If you don't have a connection, you could research the group on line. Either way, introducing yourself via email and sending a copy of your speaker profile is a good place to start finding bookings. Alternatively, you could go to local community centers and other venues to place adverts on notice boards.

Many of these groups involve retired or semi-retired people who meet on a regular basis. Generally, such events follow a similar pattern involving a combination of an official meeting during which club business is discussed, a period of time for a speaker (hopefully you) and also refreshments and social mingling. The whole event will usually last approximately two hours.

Do not make the mistake of underestimating the power of

these groups. The members are intelligent and resourceful individuals and they have contacts within all sorts of other groups. A successful talk in one group will often trigger bookings from others as your details get passed along. I found this particularly true of the Women's Institute (WI).

The WI is a multi-level membership organisation built on a foundation of WI groups set up in villages, towns and cities around the UK. They meet on a monthly basis. Every six months there are larger meetings referred to as Group Meetings. These bring together representatives from several local WIs for a number of reasons including the exchange of ideas and information. If you can speak at one of these group meetings (as I was lucky enough to do for my very first event) and that event goes well, you may well find yourself then being approached by the speaker secretaries for some of the individual WIs who had sent representatives to the Group Meeting. All of the WIs within a county come under the umbrella of that county's federation, e.g. The Hampshire County Federation of Women's Institutes (HCFWI). Above that are National Meetings.

Each WI group that meets will contain women from all walks of life, with contacts in all sorts of organisation, and very diverse interests. For example, if you have written children's books or YA fantasy/thriller, you might think that the WI wouldn't be interested in hearing about it because the individual members are not necessarily your target audience. However, if you approach your talk in the right way, they could still enjoy hearing from you. Don't forget that WI audience members are mothers, daughters, sisters, aunts, cousins, grandmothers, etc. They may well have younger relatives to buy for or recommend things to. The same goes for other social groups.

The WI speakers list

Each federation of WIs keeps an official list of good speakers which is circulated to all the local WI groups. All WI speaker secretaries refer to that list when booking the next year's speaking slots. There's an audition process for speakers who wish to be included on the list. You do not have to be a member of the WI (or a woman) to be a WI speaker. An audition for each federation is needed if you wish to appear on multiple lists. More information on auditioning for the WI speaker list is available in Appendix 2.

16

Conclusion

I hope this has given you a useful insight into public speaking as a way to have fun, promote your author platform and generate sales. And I hope that it has given you some practical information with regard to how to get started. The hints and tips I've outlined are all the things I wish I had known when I started out. There are, of course, many other books out there that will share more detailed wisdom on all aspects of public speaking. YouTube and other platforms offer advice too. It's up to you to work out what you think will work for you.

Don't forget that, if you have written a book, you have already achieved an amazing thing. You can make the leap into public speaking and if you don't want to leap, maybe just dip a toe in first and see how you get on. You have complete control over how this goes and if there are bumps in the road, you can get over them. Just take it one step at a time.

I wish you the best of luck.

Appendix 1. Speaker kit checklist

Whenever I attend a speaking event I take the following items:

- Laptop
- Connection/adapter cable
- Wireless clicker to change slides
- Projector
- Screen
- Power cable with sufficient sockets
- A box of books for sale.
- A pen to sign your books if requested.
- A float for those paying cash.
- Business cards

I also bring a few large original paintings with me. These do not get used unless my projector or computer fail to work. If that happens then I use the paintings as backup illustrations.

On many occasions, I do not need all of these things. However, knowing that I have them, just in case, helps me to feel organised. Of course, on the odd occasions that I have needed them all, I have been very glad to have them.

Appendix 2: Auditions for the WI speaker list

Based on my experience of auditioning for the WI Speakers List in 2017, the following notes might be of interest.

The purpose of the auditions for the Speakers List is to vet the vast number of people who want to speak for WI groups. This means that in order to be considered acceptable you have to be able to put together a talk that isn't going to send everyone to sleep and isn't going to be offensive or inappropriate.

The auditions process is taken very seriously. If you haven't written an interesting talk, are late, scruffy and/or patronising, you won't get approved for the speaker list. If you don't get on the list, your chances of speaking widely for multiple WIs and being recommended to other groups outside the WI in the way that I frequently am, are very limited indeed. If you are going to apply to audition, do so in earnest.

Email the Speaker Selection Secretary for your county's federation of WI's. They can tell you when the next audition is. Note that different counties' processes operate at different speeds. I had one county respond immediately to an inquiry and the other take several months to get back to me. Be patient. In the latter case, the delay wasn't due to inefficiency, but because there wasn't an upcoming audition for some months. In general, auditions take place every six months. Applicants need to express an interest in being part of the next audition. There will be a form to fill out and possibly a small administration fee to take part. If your application is successful, the speaker secretary will inform you when your audition will take place.

Expect to attend a village hall somewhere within the county at a specific time. You will be one of a number of hopeful speakers. You will not hear the other talks. At your allotted time you will be invited to come to the front of the hall and give a short sample of your talk, lasting approximately 15 minutes, enough to give a taster of what it is about and why they might want to hear the whole thing. This will enable the audience to be able to judge if you are suitable to be approved for the list.

They will be looking for several factors. Some of these might include:

- Organisation. Did you arrive on time?
- Efficiency. Could you set up any equipment and clear away promptly? Did you have any IT issues? Could you solve them without it causing major problems? Did you have a backup plan if your computer/ projector failed?
- Clarity. When you speak are you loud enough and clear enough to be heard? Can you use a microphone, if needed?
- Interest. Is the talk engaging? Does it make the listener want to hear more?
- Suitability. Is the talk appropriate? Avoid the obvious;

swearing, blasphemy etc. It's possible to talk about difficult subjects as long as it is done with respect and decency for all involved.

The audience members will vote on each applicant. Those deemed acceptable will be offered the opportunity to join the list. There will be another form to fill in and an annual fee for administration. Once on the list, your details will be circulated to all WIs within that federation.

Every year, when the list is updated, you will be asked if you wish to pay an additional administration fee to stay on the list.

About the author - Alice G May

As a direct result of the real story behind The House That Sat Down (our house really did fall down), I gave up my twenty-year career in the NHS and became a part-time school librarian whilst building my writing and speaking business. Three years later, I became a full-time freelance writer, artist and speaker.

I present regularly on the importance of building positive mental health and resilience through self-care and creative activities. I also talk about writing, painting and speaking to anyone who looks remotely interested, so watch out. Details of my talks can be found on my website, www.alicegmay.com.

I am mother to four (not-so-small-anymore) children and I am fortunate enough to be married to probably (or so *he* says) the most patient man on the planet. We live in, what used to be, a ramshackle old cottage in the country.

I hope you have found this book useful, enjoyable, and/or incredibly effective as a paperweight or doorstop. Whichever it is, please leave a review, I'd be delighted to see it.

Many thanks.

Alice x

Other links:

- Twitter: @AliceMay_Author
- Instagram: @alicegmay
- LinkedIn: Alice May
- Facebook: AliceMayAuthor

Alternatively, you can see me painting on YouTube by searching for 'Alice May Artist'.

The House That Sat Down Trilogy by Alice May is available on Amazon as both Kindle and paperback.

Acknowledgements

My heartfelt thanks to all the amazing clubs and groups that have invited me to speak for them over the last eight years, and all the incredible, inspiring people I have meet at these events. Your kind welcome, encouragement and feedback have helped me to grow as a speaker and I am hugely grateful.

Thank you to my wonderful parents for — whenever I say to them, 'I've just had a great idea for a book,' — not rolling their eyes, dropping their heads in their hands or groaning as if in serious pain. Instead, they look genuinely interested. They could simply be excellent actors, but I like to think not. They are definitely biased, though, and I love them for it. Similarly, a huge cheer goes to my husband and children for their endless patience. Thank you all for the hours spent beta reading, proof reading and making useful suggestions.

Finally, thank you to Elane and Sarah (co-founders of www.iaminprint.co.uk) and the member of *The Writing Sphere*. Without your encouragement (and Scott Pack's awesome tutorials on editing, of course) this book never have made it into print.

It's all about ...n good

Jelly und Just one

...re time!

Printed in Great Britain
by Amazon

21215933R00047